NORTH AMERICAN ANIMALS

AMERICAN BISON

by Jill Sherman

AMICUS | AMICUS INK

Amicus High Interest and Amicus Ink are imprints of Amicus
P.O. Box 1329, Mankato, MN 56002
www.amicuspublishing.us

Library of Congress Cataloging-in-Publication Data
Names: Sherman, Jill., author.
Title: American bison / by Jill Sherman.
Description: Mankato, Minnesota : Amicus/Amicus Ink, [2019] | Series: North American animals | Audience: K to grade 3. | Includes bibliographical references and index.
Identifiers: LCCN 2017047814 (print) | LCCN 2017049491 (ebook) | ISBN 9781681514949 (pdf) | ISBN 9781681514123 (library binding) | ISBN 9781681523323 (pbk.)
Subjects: LCSH: American bison--Juvenile literature.
Classification: LCC QL737.U53 (ebook) | LCC QL737.U53 S4825 2019 (print) | DDC 599.64/3--dc23
LC record available at https://lccn.loc.gov/2017047814

Photo Credits: Doug Lindstrand/Design Pics Inc/Alamy Stock Photo cover; GlobalP/iStock 2; Neal Herbert/Yellowstone National Park/Flickr 4–5; John E Marriott/Getty 6–7; Don White/SuperStock/Alamy Stock Photo 8–9; JohanWElzenga/iStock 10–11; Nina B/Shutterstock 12–13; Dancingdice/Shutterstock 14; Mike Cavaroc/Alamy 16–17; John Mix Stanley/Smithsonian American Art Museum/WikiCommons 18–19; Joel Sartore/NatGeo 20–21; Isselee/Dreamstime 22

Editor: Wendy Dieker
Designer: Aubrey Harper
Photo Researcher: Holly Young

Printed in China

HC 10 9 8 7 6 5 4 3 2 1
PB 10 9 8 7 6 5 4 3 2 1

TABLE OF CONTENTS

HOME ON THE RANGE

The Great Plains of North America is home to American bison **herds**. These large **mammals** roam the grasslands. They **graze** on grass, herbs, shrubs, and twigs.

OVER THE HUMP

Bison are the biggest land animals in North America. They have huge, humped backs. They grow long, furry manes. Horns grow from their large heads.

SAFETY IN NUMBERS

Few animals hunt bison. But herds help bison stay safe. A pack of wolves may attack a lone bison. To stay watchful for danger, bison only sleep for 2 to 10 minutes at a time.

Check This Out

Bison may also find safety by taking cover in lakes or rivers.

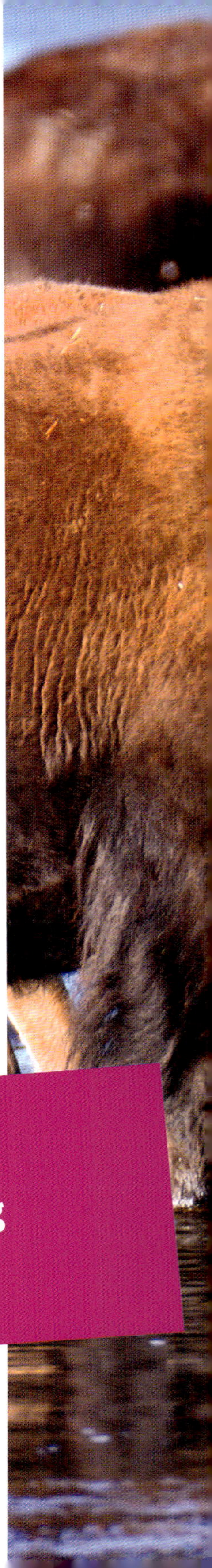

STAMPEDE!

A bison senses danger. It lets out a loud snort. The herd takes off running. It's a **stampede**! American bison can run 40 miles (64 km) per hour. They can run together for miles.

SET IN MOTION

Bison are almost always moving. The herd moves together to find more food. They don't stay still for very long. They even move while they eat!

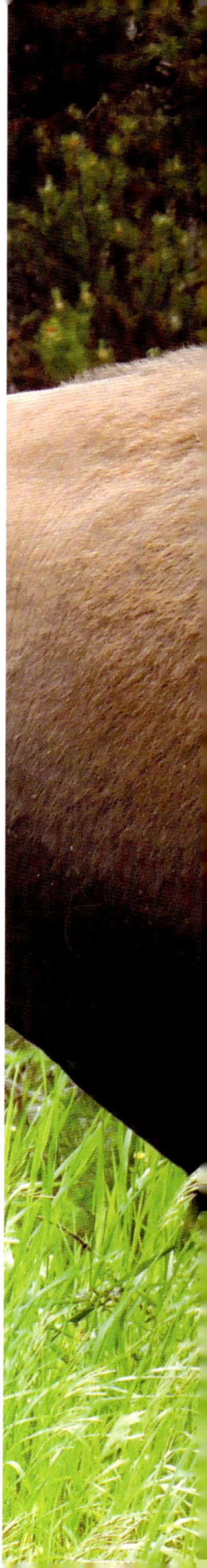

FAMILY LIFE

Groups of 10 to 20 American bison live together. **Bulls** live in one herd. **Cows** and calves live in another. Bulls and cows come together in the summer to **breed**.

LOCKING HORNS

Cows pick their **mates**. The bulls compete for attention. They ram heads. They push with their horns. They follow a cow until she chooses a mate. Calves are born the next spring.

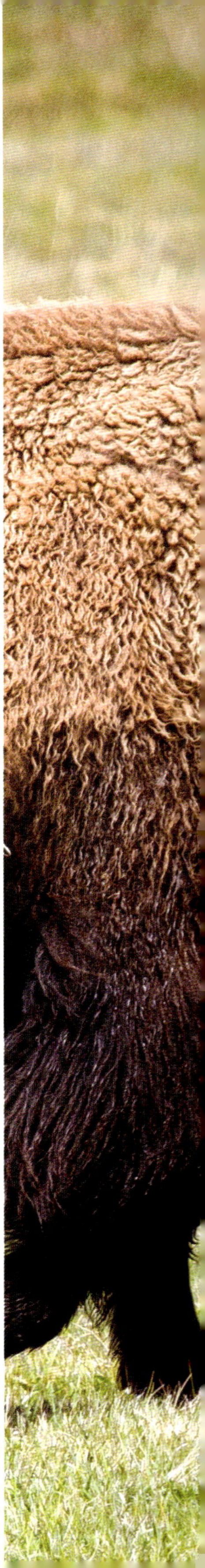

ROAMING FREE

Once, there were millions of American bison. Plains Indians relied on bison for food. Bison were central to their way of life. In the late 1800s, white settlers hunted bison for sport. Very few bison were left.

Check This Out

Early French fur trappers mistakenly called bison "buffalo." The name has stuck.

BACK FROM THE BRINK

Today, bison live in protected areas. About 30,000 wild bison roam in parks and reserves. About 500,000 more live on farms and ranches. Someday the Great Plains may have many more bison.

A LOOK AT AMERICAN BISON

WORDS TO KNOW

breed – to come together to produce young.

bull – a male bison.

cow – a female bison.

graze – to continually eat grass in a field.

herd – a group of animals that lives and moves together.

mate – a male or female in a pair of animals that comes together to produce young.

mammal – a warm-blooded animal with hair that feeds milk to its young.

stampede – when a herd of animals runs together to escape danger.

LEARN MORE

Books

Hansen, Grace. *American Bison*. Animals of North America. Edina, MN: ABDO Publishing. 2016.

Morlock, Theresa. *The Return of the American Bison*. Bouncing back from extinction. New York: PowerKids Press, 2018.

Websites

American Prairie Reserve: Bison Restoration
https://www.americanprairie.org/project/bison-restoration

National Geographic Kids: American Bison
http://kids.nationalgeographic.com/animals/american-bison/

INDEX